AF455145

Divine Intercourse: A Manifesto of the Soul

Divine Intercourse: A Manifesto of the Soul

Brother Jason

Jesus Christ and His Sermon on the Mount

Matthew 5-7

Jason David Jones
2013

Copyright © 2013 by Jason David Jones

All rights reserved. This book or any portion thereof may not be reproduced or used in any manner whatsoever without the express written permission of the publisher except for the use of brief quotations in a book review or scholarly journal.

First Printing: 2013

ISBN 978-1-304-70184-8

Jason David Jones
Box 1967
Beaverlodge, Alberta, Canada T0H 0C0

Dedication

To my Lord and Saviour, Jesus Christ, who allowed His body to be broken for the forgiveness of my sins, allowing a new attitude to wash over my soul.

Contents

Preface

Divine
Addressed, appropriated, or devoted to God

Intercourse
Communication or dealings between individuals or groups

Manifesto
A public declaration of policy and aims

Soul
The non-physical part of a person which is the seat of emotions and character

Introduction

This message is one of revelation, not one of judgmental demands. It is one that has been lost on the hearts of God's church. Not in the sense of the "Christian Church" but in the broader sense of "God's Church". God's Church is the entire created world around us, every corner dark or lit. Everyone saved or unsaved, Jew or Gentile. This message of revelation is meant to be a benefit to all people seeking to be prosperous in their life, in love or fellowship. This is Christ's message of example to His brother and sisters.

Above all; this is a message of peace, understanding and compassion. This message is framed around communication, communication of the soul with the world. For too long Christianity has focused on man-made doctrines leading to a manufactured faith. Christ encourages us to live by a faith, exampled by His character.

Teaching a life of man-made doctrine is to teach falsely. Christ teaches us a spiritual faith that opens the doors of forgiveness to all those who seek it. No matter the current situation of our soul, forgiveness is free and unconditional. If one truly is seeking a Christian life, one must live by the example of Christ. Jesus' character can have an enormous effect on a seekers life if truly embraced, exampled in both heart and soul. Living the revealing will of God is what Jesus encourages us to do through His example. His miracles are a testament to living a life of healing, salvation and amazement. We all, to some point, have mastered the miracle of salvation. Accepting the holiness of Jesus and His redeeming love saves us from the eternal death awaiting us.

Meditating and praying on the Word of God maintains the blessing bestowed unto us by the Lord. We must move on from Calvary beginning the journey of faith, choosing to be filled not just saved. Christ's words are an amazing well of Spiritual Truths, directed by God. If we saturate our lives with the Word, our souls will reflect the life of Christ.

Our minds control our actions; if our minds are true to the Word we will have an abundant righteous life. Unfortunately, if our minds harbor negative, discouraging thoughts our actions will reflect it. Jesus' life reflects this truth, as He carried the testimony of peace and joy where ever He went. Never forgetting; that the very Son of God was Himself betrayed onto death. He faced this determined course with faith in His all-knowing God and Father. Our minds are our dominion, mastered only after one has tamed their souls. Once we train our souls, maintaining them accordingly; we will have control over our physical lives. God gave us free will; our free will starts with the renewing of our thoughts.

Accepting spiritual truths is the first step to mastering our minds and thoughts. Even Jesus had free will, He was free to embrace God's will and free to stray from it. Jesus mastered His soul, by doing so He was able to prove everything He professed. When we follow the leading of the Spirit, overcoming obstacles we please God, blessing all mankind.

Jesus realized the spiritual hunger of His brothers and sisters, so he decided to share His wisdom, inviting all people of all walks of life. Christ shared this wisdom as revealed in the Sermon of the Mount. These teachings of Christ, if applied to every aspect of life, can offer aid in the overcoming of religious strongholds. His teachings can have an immediate effect if applied wholeheartedly. Jesus gives us a blueprint to become a master of the Soul through a peaceful understanding of the surrounding world.

Empowerment

Spiritual poverty turns our own prideful way of life, desiring the need for a higher power. A higher calling and direction in life, spiritual poverty creates selfishness. Releasing our souls from habitual prejudices and worldly thoughts only happens when we accept the riches of a loving God.

Jesus teaches us to shed the hierarchy of worldly honor and degrees. This teaching encourages us all to be equal in each other's eyes. When we become equal to one another, judgmental hatred has no opportunity to mature.

The submission of our souls to God, allows Him to influence our life's desires. The Holy Spirit can guide us away from the teachings of the world.

The world is dismantling the very foundation of our souls. We must ask ourselves, are we willing to submit to the Lord our God? Are we willing to step away from our positions of authority? Above all, are we as Christians willing to leave judgment to God, choosing to love instead?

Jesus knew it would take painful sorrow to hear the sweat whisperings of God. On our knees we become completely submitted to the Lord, emptied of selfish pride. If we search out God, before falling to a point of loss, we will have a far more fulfilling life.

We must seek the power of God before we become ill, before we go broke. We must be on our knees before sorrow hits, acknowledging His overwhelming sovereignty over our lives.

Praying before God for His blessed guidance is our Christian duty, as well as our privilege. Most of us have become spoiled in the Lord, coming before God with no offering in hand. We must always come to the Lord's altar with a sacrifice of praise. Whether it is thankful forgiveness or unconditional love, we must leave something for our Father to delight in.

We must pray as a servant would serve his master. A good servant tends to his master's desire; our master desires companionship with His creation. Praying every day can help avoid future sorrow, creating peace in our Spirit.

In prayerful meditation, the word “earth” becomes our whole physical experience. Inheriting the earth happens when we create successful harmony in our physical life. Walking on water was possible with enough faith, yet taken away in a second of doubt.

Submission

Becoming meek, we must be faithfully devoted to God. We must honor our Father as the Good Son would. This attitude allows us the privilege of knowing the blessing of a loving Father. We must allow only God the position of judgment.

We are to be lovingly faithful to all those who seek the love of our Father. As meek children of God, we must seek no judgment against our brothers or sisters. We must instead concern ourselves with our own faithful obedience to God. We must strive to live our lives, walking on water.

To be righteous, we must be right in our thoughtful conduct regarding our entire influence. Our thoughts conduct all our actions. If we have negative thoughts we cannot have positive interactions with our physical surroundings.

If we want to be healed, we must first think it is possible and then faithfully decide to be healed. We must allow only peaceful contentment to occupy our thoughts. If we want to be prosperous, we must first think it is the will of God and then faithfully pursue it. If we want to be loved, we must first think it is possible for someone to love us and then allow ourselves to be loved.

Our thoughts are the catalyst to choosing a faithful life opposed to a carnal one. If we choose to adopt positive thoughts, as Jesus did, we will soon see the positive changes around us.

Society has conditioned us to rely on our physical decision making processes. When we turn to anger or wrath, we may feel the urge to hurt someone, playing it out in our thoughts. Many of us realize it is wrong to hurt another, choosing divinity over carnality. Unfortunately, the simple thought of hurting someone is more dangerous to our spiritual peace than the physical act.

Everything we are accustomed to have control over is on a physical plane. We gain control over our physical lives by manually choosing to do so. We manually push the right button in the elevator, taking us to the desired floor. We control our entire worldly experience to a point of disaster, condemning ourselves to an experience of stagnant confinement.

We begin to plateau in our maturity, we no longer feel challenged or we feel challenged to a point of constant failure. We have either fitted the costume of Christianity or don't feel right wearing it.

Our flesh, our outward experience, becomes our constant focus. All of our energy, focused on a historically losing area of faith. We desire outward change, neglecting our inward needs. The needs of the soul are what matters in the transformation of a lasting form. We must desire to change inwardly, acknowledging it will take much time.

Perspective

It is easy for us to live out our entire true selves in our minds, carrying judgmental negativity wherever we go, even into our Churches. Like a Trojan horse our lives become a tool for evil instead of good.

It is so easy to adorn the costume of Christianity, yet never embrace Christ nor ever feel forgiving peace.

Our thoughts are not confined to the law of time. We are free to daydream about the past, about the future. We are not confined in our thoughts to the laws of our land. We are free to lust, murder or steal. We have the freedom to safeguard our true desires, hiding our real self. This has been the way of all humanity. God is the only one who has full access to our true identities.

Positive, harmonious thoughts are the basis to affecting a Christ-like inward change. We must turn to peace in our thoughts, no longer choosing self-righteousness over Godly obedience. Peace is only possible when we choose harmony over self.

Jesus exampled this great truth to us, for as the very child of God, never did He condemn another. Jesus always choose harmonious peace over selfish desire. Even while upon the cross He did not cast judgmental hatred upon His persecutors. Our Lord's character is the way to eternal life, to reflect Him tears down strongholds.

We are not required to change overnight; only abandon the life of the flesh. Abandon our worldly influences, choosing an inward life lead by the Holy Spirit. By living an inward life we can truly claim a lasting victory in the name of our Lord Jesus.

Forgiveness, resentment, jealousy and hatred are our starting points. Working through these burdens will take a great deal of courageous maturity.

Mercy

If we claim each victory in the name of God, in the pursuit of peace, we will be filled with righteousness crowned with humility. Claiming the presence of the Father in every corner of our soul, we must expose any negative presence. Once exposed, we must replace the negativity with the Lord's righteous peace.

Mercy becomes the character of righteousness in our life, only if carried out in our soul first. Acts of kindness are hypocritical when those acts are clouded by unkind thoughts. We must desire to be merciful not just appear to mimic mercy. The body of Christ is to be merciful, therefore; reserve judgment, especially mindful judgment, for God and God alone. Our mercy must be used to help our brothers or sisters to a life of the soul.

We must not dwell on the outward experiences, as they are only an indication of an inner burden. When backsliding or sinfulness arises among our brothers or sisters, the Holy Spirit is crying out for our help. This cry calls us to act in merciful compassion, in order to build up the fellowship.

We must no longer condemn, for if we act in a spirit of mercy, we will encourage those weaker to become stronger. We are all members of the Body of Christ, all needing mercy bestowed upon us. If we refuse mercy to another in need, then we too will find ourselves abandoned when we find ourselves in need.

Many of us envision God as an earthly father, limited by physical boundaries, limited to three dimensions. God is limitless, boundless and omnipresent. When we limit God to three dimensions, we limit His dominion along with our Spiritual lives to the same. Christ is our narrow gate to God's fourth dimension. God is our fourth dimension, or Kingdom on Earth; He is a whole other life experience. When we finally realize this, we will then begin to see the Kingdom of Heaven working around us and through us.

When we completely embrace this revelation, no longer living three dimensionally, our soul will yearn to be brought into alignment with God's will. Our soul will begin to reflect His peaceful love, viewing the world around us through His eyes. We will yearn to be merciful, lusting to see God at work in the lives of others.

As an addict trapped in the world three dimensionally is driven to seek out a physical fulfillment to the burden of desire. We as children of our fourth dimensional Father, known as Jesus, need only seek the spiritual fulfillment of the Kingdom of Heaven.

The spirit of peace, or serenity, is a foundational truth that must be sought after and nurtured. If we desire any lasting change within our soul we need to seek the Kingdom within. Forgiveness, fear, resentment are all necessary areas of spiritual attention.

To overcome these stumbling blocks we must fall to our knees prayerfully in communion with God. Jesus, when faced with fearful hardships, relied heavily on His open companionship with God. God is the only way to lasting merciful peace. Only when we live in constant fellowship with God do we truly become connected to the power of the Holy Spirit.

We will never have peace on earth by way of man. We will have peace, however; by way of God within our soul. Committing to peace means submitting to God's will for our soul.

We can only become peacemakers by first attending to the condition of our soul. Only when our motives are reflective of an eternal inner peace will we have an opportunity to affect an outward peace.

Persecution

Many of our faithful Pastors are being persecuted for preaching messages in alignment with God's will, not aligning themselves with the elders or congregation. Self-righteous elders who live a physical religion are forcing our pastors out of the Church. If these elders were to only concern themselves with the condition of their own souls, then they would gain a more thorough understanding of the teachings of Christ.

We need to allow ourselves to be persecuted in the name of righteousness. We must not allow ourselves to hold self-serving habitual thoughts. We must empty our self of personal character, allowing God control of our soul. Persecution in the name of God, is never allowing our faith to be compromised by another person. Many of us fall prey to compromise, hoping to salvage a small sense of Christianity.

Limiting persecution to the physical sense, in definition, is a misguided confinement. Persecution within God's church will come in ways of self-serving judgments and compromised doctrines. The persecutions we will face can extinguish the fire of God in a moment, leaving us morally stripped trapped in desolation. Persecution will come our way as soon as we accept Jesus Christ into our hearts.

When we accept Jesus Christ into our lives, we bring forward our souls out from darkness. Doing so, the very essence of who we are is placed upon a mountain top for all to see. Our personal lives, along with the condition of our souls, become the center focus of everyone around us. When we share our Christian beliefs with others, they will begin to draw judgmental comparisons all in the name of fear. This is the persecution God has counted us worthy to bare.

If we wish to remain victorious in our peaceful faith, we must make every effort to destroy our own judgmental persecutory nature. We must polish our vessel so our light can shine from within, lighting miles from the mountaintop.

Transformation

The natural desires of selfishness, pride, hate, jealousy, prejudice, resentment and most importantly self-righteousness. All of the desires of our flesh must be starved from our souls, releasing their control which will allow us to choose a life of faithful prayer. Resisting the natural impulse to feed our flesh desire will starve the old self from within, allowing the new self to shine forth. Offering blessed, merciful thoughts or actions to all people God puts in our path; that is how we represent a true child of God.

If we follow through consistently without wavering, our peaceful influence will be echoed through generations. Reaching nations we will never visit, touching people we will never meet in a positive, peaceful, spiritual way. Jesus is proof of this truth. Our brother in God's family left His spiritual mark using mercy and peace. He is a bright light in a time of darkness. We have an opportunity and privilege to follow his example.

If we want to be counted as a Christian, our souls must reflect a peaceful and merciful servant of God. We need not be perfect for that would lead to boastfulness. We must only desire to be perfected by living out our lives in reflection of Christ-like character. God works out the kinks as we mature, growing spiritually.

Examination

If we are struggling physically, we need only examine ourselves inwardly. For God has made us uniquely in a way, that our soul will balance out our flesh not allowing our flesh to overtake our soul. Lasting spiritual growth will only happen from the inner stronghold of our soul outward. The maturing of our soul is centered squarely on our personal relationship with the Lord Jesus Christ. Our personal relationship with Jesus is only nurtured through a consistent prayer life.

Our personal relationship is a private inward life that we must not force on anyone. For it would be like scorning a small baby for not having adult wisdom. We are responsible for the condition of our own, individual souls. We as children of God must pray without ceasing for those who struggle in maturity, loving them continually with an understanding patience. We as children of God need only reflect the harmonious life of Christ. If we bring harmonious peace to our souls, others will desire the wonderful Christian blessing.

We are cities upon hilltops, lights shining with welcome mats rolled out. Love, peace, and mercy are our tourist attractions. Never lose sight of our true purpose here on earth. We are here to aggressively win souls to the Kingdom of the Almighty God! This aggression is not to be focused on the pre-Christian; it is to be focused directly on the enemy. Our weapons are prayer and fasting ensuring an empowered offensive attack against the enemy. Love, peace, and mercy are our tools in this ministry which ensure we do not push the young in faith into a life of spiritual torment.

True Christianity, as taught by Christ, is truly wonderful and positive. It is to be a rewarding and encouraging life, not a restrictive one. Knowingly accepting Christ into our lives puts us at a higher responsibility to carry out the great commission. We are to rise above mere physical morality, challenging our spiritual morality. We need to embrace the Christian life, battling our inner weaknesses, replacing them with the Light of Truth.

Confining others to a physical moral life offers us up to the judgment of God. We need to see everyone with eyes of mercy, love and peace. If we do not, we are not honoring our Father, our Brother or our Soul. We need to represent Christianity as a spiritual choice, not a religion. Confinement to a life of physical laws and rituals, binds our faith; making it no different than any other religion. Within the Christian spiritual faith we can finally feel secure in our beliefs, as well; happy in our physical life.

Our spiritual faith will enable us to continue our desired search for personal perfection. We need not forgo our spiritual maturing because we do not meet a set of physical moral laws. The Christian faith is not determined by only what we do, additionally; it is determined by what we feel and think. As soon as a temptation enters our mind, we must pray for God's help aloud. We must put the responsibility of our perfection in His hands.

Failure

When we fail, falling prey to our tempting thoughts, we must get up and try again. Over and over if we must, praying faithfully for deliverance. God will answer us, releasing us from the enemy's continuous attacks. Facing morality in this way is the only way to claim victory over our sinfulness. Trying to do so by mere physical will-power or abstention sets us up for future fall.

When we pray, all we must do is remember God wants to help us, temptations have no power over us, and our souls are perfectly blessed by the sanctifying blood of Jesus Christ. Realizing that the more spiritual knowledge we possess the greater our fall when we error in our morality. As Christians we must be more careful to adhere to morality in every aspect of our life. If we allow the enemy a foothold of any kind in our life he will immediately take up residence. God loves us, forgiving us of our weakness, all He asks is we continue on our path to a righteous Christ-like reflection.

Sovereignty

The Bible is the inherent word of God, infallible and inspired. It is a testimony to God's sovereignty and love. The Old Law was established to forge a sense of morality in an otherwise perverse and barbaric world. If we truly reflect on this truth we will realize that regardless of our faith; we know murder, theft, adultery and untruthfulness to be all immoral. It is hard wired into our being. Even people, who claim to have no faith in any one god or higher power, know these basic moral wrongs. God taught an entire world the value of right and wrong, good and evil, life and death.

Some may argue that there are a select few who mentally cannot differentiate between right and wrong. These unfortunate beings are the lost few that have refused the teaching of these basic moral laws. All of us are under the judgment of life and death. Moral laws, that most of our countries have adapted to judge civility among the population. This truth must be recognized as a declaration that our God is the King of kings. For in the life of Jesus Christ we see a pure example of this morality, the absolute sovereignty of God. Jesus exampled every day what it was to be a living, successful child of our God.

The New Testament lays the foundation for us to complete our entire being. As man matured, becoming masters of the basic physical laws of the Old Testament, they attempted to add to and of course alter the Laws. This allowed the religious few to segregate and judge the multitude. Man was so comfortable with their understanding of physical morality they attempted to distort its borders. The addition of customs and traditions clouded this truth. God then exposed a further set of moral Laws, no longer physical but spiritual.

The teachings of Christ attempt to set a new course of enlightenment. Jesus shows us the next step we must take. We must acknowledge our inner spirituality while still observing the Old Law. No longer is it good enough to abstain from murder, for Christ teaches us that harboring angry thoughts is equally sinful. If we fail, becoming angry with another, we must seek forgiveness and cleansing. This truth applied in our lives will lead to a peaceful spirit. To be angry with our brother or sister is sufficient cause for God to withhold the blessing of peaceful contentment in our life. Just as a vinedresser removes the dead or infected branches in the vineyard, so must we prune our spiritual immorality and emotional bondage.

Until we master our resentful judgment of our fellow man, God will not reveal the true power of prayer or peace. God will not allow any great healings or spiritual powers to enter into the dominion of our soul. God will deny us Heaven on Earth; choose pride or peace, not both. Christ is the Prince of Peace not the Prince of Pride.

Peaceful souls are productive souls. We must offer up our negative prejudices, resentments and wrathful emotions to God.

Offer them as our sacrificial burnt offerings. The Old Law focuses on a physical offering when seeking God's forgiveness or praise. The New Law focuses on spiritual morality, seeking a spiritual or emotional offering.

Jesus showed us a truly peaceful attitude towards all people. Christ met all walks of life with respect and love. At sometimes it may have been a curt respect, respect nonetheless. God placed Jesus among all classes of society, saints or sinners, Jesus witnessed to them all. Setting an ultimate example for His Church to model and reflect. Jesus was able to carry out this will of God, by offering all His prejudicial, sinful thoughts to God as His continual, daily sacrifice.

Christ teaches us to accept every single man or woman on this earth as children of our Almighty Father. Counting everyone worthy of His love, it is not our place to judge. We are encouraged, even commanded, to lovingly forgive all His children, growing into a peaceful understanding. To count anyone a fool, unworthy or useless, elevates us to the very seat of the judge. Into the judgment seat we challenge the sovereign authority of God.

The only way to overcome the temptation to judge another is to be in constant prayer. We are commanded by God to empty ourselves before communing with Him in prayer. So before we pray, let us take inventory of our judgments, anger and hatred; releasing them to God. Once we have done this we can continue our prayer, which will be empowered by our peaceful attitude. Once we have truly sacrificed our prejudicial thoughts we become blank slates, a willing tool in the hand of God.

If we are on the offensive when faced with temptations we will be prepared to repel Satan, never allowing him a foothold within our soul. If we are on the defensive, Satan will gain entrance into our soul, leaving us the task of removing him. As Christians we are to be offensive in our faith, never caught off guard. Standing hand-in-hand with the mighty warrior that is Jesus Christ. Being on the offensive prepares us to deal with worldly emotional influences, releasing us from many draining burdens. We must seek God prayerfully, facing every worldly influence offensively.

Jesus drives home the fact that our thoughts are real dangers when He commands us not to commit adultery in our hearts. If lusting after another is the same as a physical act of immoral intercourse, the same must be true for all our thoughts. We must guard our thoughts well, being constantly on the spiritual offensive.

Jesus wants us to embrace this truth, for if our thoughts can become a negative bondage they also can offer us a positive freedom. If our thoughts, or habits, can lead us to open sin then they can also lead us to physical blessings. If our covetous thoughts lead us to eventually steal, then our healing thoughts can lead us to renewed health. Our free will is ours to guide and use. We must focus our hearts on positive distractions, not negative ones.

In order to experience all the wonderful blessings awaiting us, we must nurture and mature our soul. We must thrust ourselves, completely into a life of God and forgiveness. Our soul must be our first and greatest concern. We must not allow any compromising of our souls. If we know of sinfulness within our soul we must remove it, at whatever cost. If we want an open relationship with God we must first want our soul to be clean of prideful hatred, along with all negative fruits. Jesus taught us to seek righteousness if we want blessing.

Marriage

Jesus further teaches us to be humble in marriage. He challenges us to see with eyes of love, not entitlement or ownership. This is to say, all our marital challenges need to be met from the other's point of view. We are to challenge our desire to separate or divorce. If we put God in the center of our marital quarrels we will begin to conduct ourselves with a spirit of peaceful love.

Divorce is not to be taken lightly; it will compel us to a life of continued disappointment in other relationships. Failing to resolve marital problems, fails to correct the real underlying problems, transferring them to our new marital relationship.

Too many times we expect our spouses to come into alignment with our own desires which we feel entitled to. We expect our better half to become our lesser half. This expectation leads to a master-servant relationship instead of a husband-wife partnership. We must acknowledge each other as equals, with much to teach and learn within the union of marriage.

Today's marriages are failing for the simple fact that we are not willing to admit we are fallible and imperfect. God wants us to learn from each other, becoming spiritually intimate growing together in intercourse. Refusing to set aside our pride is what hinders us from having a fulfilling relationship.

Divorce should never be a better option than accepting a portion of humility. The condition of our marriage directly reflects the condition of our soul. Divorce should only be considered if there be unrepentant evil darkening a marriage, subjecting one to dangers. God is just and forgiving, which allows for us to assure our safety. Only if one is in an adulterous or dangerous marriage is it acceptable to adopt a spirit of divorce. Search your heart for God's guidance in the matters of marital decisions.

Divorce carries a great spiritual burden of reconditioning self-discovery so as not to fall prey again to the same torment. Learn from marriage, journey together in loving humility that will encourage mutual growth. If divorced, acknowledge the attitudes of entitlement that lead to the dissolving of the union, repent and turn from them before remarriage.

Oaths

An oath can bind us to a life of doctrinal bondage. Jesus teaches us that compelling ourselves in the name of God to uphold a defined set of doctrines, manipulated by man is bonding and disrespectful.

Bonding, as it no longer allows the free movement of the Holy Spirit to direct us in God's will. We become slaves of a denominational church, not a servant of God's sovereign church. God should be our master with the freedom to guide us as He pleases. A pathway of denominational doctrines refuses the Holy Spirit control of our lives.

Disrespectful, for God alone created us to do His will; not the will of our denominational church. The church is the Body of Christ, therefore; the church should be the servant to the Master. As with our own physical bodies hearing, seeing, smelling, sustenance, thought and impulse all come from the head. Our spiritual church bodies should look to the head, Jesus Christ, for this same guidance and submission.

Such oaths of bondage are compelling our ministers to serve the will of the denominational church, not God's church. Doctrinal oaths have lead to frustrated stagnation within our once glorious church bodies, resonating throughout all their ministries. Churches have become paralyzed from the neck down due to confining doctrines, forcing Christians to take a side. We must not allow compromising oaths to control the will of God's church, above all; our individual spiritual growth. Oaths that uphold doctrine over faith are simply unacceptable in the sight of God.

Oaths that facilitate daily life are of no concern to God, as they will die with our bodies. Oaths of truth in courts of law, contractual oats and personal promises are of no concern to God. For if we are living a life of truth the result of these oaths will be a truthful testimony. If we fail to honor any one of these oaths, forgiveness is assured if we seek it out with a repentant heart. In contrast, if we deny the Holy Spirit freedom in our lives by way of doctrinal oaths we find forgiveness to be unattainable. We must not allow our life of faith to be compromised by a life of the flesh.

Brother Jason

Grace

Turning the other cheek is Jesus' way of laying a foundation of change. For we as barbarians were taught by the Old Law to settle accounts through a blood sacrifice.

Jesus now asks us to hold ourselves to a higher spiritual accountability. When we are wronged, our carnal nature is to seek restitution. This barbaric response leads to a sense of hate-filled revenge. Jesus wishes us to turn the other cheek, choosing no longer to instinctively seek revenge or retaliation. He wants us to instead react in a spirit of peaceful understanding. We have a chance to end the cycle of trespass.

Turning the other cheek requires great restraining strength at first, leading later to a habit graceful peace. Jesus does not wish us to be cowards; only hold ourselves accountable to a higher standard of grace. Turning the other cheek is the conscious decision to deny our carnal selves when facing a hurtful trespass, choosing a mature attitude of peace exampling the Son of God.

This will not only change your life but your enemy's as well. Turning the other cheek stops the cycle of vengeful hatred. Peace is the product of a graceful understanding. We must allow our fellowman his attitudes and beliefs. We must not fall prey to foolishness, allowing concession on all unessential points. We must only focus our disagreements on matters of God and His truth. Everything else is unimportant when considering eternity. If a trespasser is faced with righteousness, they will change their path avoiding those who do not feed their desire for disrupting hate. Anyone can avenge a trespass; only a Child of God can have the capacity to livingly forgive. Turn the other cheek, stop hate with a choice.

Jesus directs us to love our enemies. He reveals to us that it is very easy to lovingly forgive those who lovingly forgive us. We must be encouraged to the extra mile. We must forgive those who we consider our enemies. We are to do this in order to encourage them to change their ways. By forgiving we are telling them it is okay to fall from grace, as we have all one time or another.

We must search out the lost lambs, not abandoning them to be prey for the wolves. Too many times our churches neglect the hopeless sinners that truly desire forgiveness and truth. Sometimes we are too quick to pass judgment on the less desirables or hard cases of this world. We would rather invest our efforts on confusing doctrine, repelling those who are in the true need of God's grace; ultimately challenging those who do not fall in line with misguided denominational beliefs.

When we meet evil with evil, we give it more power, strengthening the hold it has over the person it inhabits. If we respond to evil with love, we break the cycle, destroying its hold on our enemies. If we forgive, we appeal to the Christ desire within that everyone yearns to fulfill. We as the body of Christ must accept the lost, lovingly forgiving them. If we must forgive them continually on a daily basis, then that is what must be done. Such as the army did unto Jericho, when called by our

Supreme Commander the Lord God, we must persevere serving his directional will.

It is God's privilege to forsake and judge, not ours. When we fear something we are giving it power over our faith. We must use our faith to be continuously victorious. When we as a church entertain fear, we give it power to divide us from the blessing of a multiplying faith. Christ did not consume His efforts on earth with judgment nor condemnation; He focused on forgiving in love. God's plan for the church is for us to carry out what Christ started. Loving your enemies accomplishes two divine tasks.

First, it compels our enemies to consider change, seeing the truth in the teachings of Christ. If we as Christians (little Christ) will only embrace our own teachings; living in love we reveal to our enemies the power of our forgiving God. When we interact with evil in a divine way, our enemies will see a greater value in our faith. When we live this principle out we truly become the salt to this earth.

If we love our homosexual brothers and sisters, as we do our straight siblings, we will have more meaningful dialogue. If we love our incarcerated, forgiving them of their mistakes, then maybe we could truly impact their lives for good. If we forgave our trespassers immediately, we wouldn't waste our lives living out past transgressions and stereotypes. Instead, we would be free to live out our future interactions un-burdened and truly free in Christ.

Second, forgiving our enemies will lead to a better life for us. We cannot have peace in our life if we have hate in our heart. No matter our distracted sibling's choices on their pathway through life we must grow to accept them as another sheep in Christ's flock, acknowledging some are lost, needing to be reclaimed. We need only remind ourselves that at one time or another we were all lost, in need of an accepting love.

We must pray for the lost children God puts us in contact with, for He does so for a reason. Prayer with a faithful, peaceful heart will change lives.

Jesus commands us to storm the gates of Heaven. We must arise from our doctrinal slumbers, taking hold of the very tangible Kingdom of God. The Kingdom of God is there for our taking. Whatever our affliction, all we must do is repent wholeheartedly, seek God's forgiveness, and accept that forgiveness into our lives. An eternal, perfected life lies awaiting our taking.

We are not asked to become perfect overnight, as some of our churches require. We need only to have the desire to grow in Christ, learning to accept children of God regardless of their transgressions. Love and forgiveness are our tools for constructing an eternal life. We must decide now, today. Going to bed without choosing the Kingdom of God today, gives evil hatred another day to reign in our life.

We are all children of God, whether we have decided or not. We must decide which kingdom we wish to help build. Do we desire to help build a kingdom that is founded on a forgiving, peaceful love; or do we wish to help build a kingdom that is founded on a dividing, hateful destruction.

Decide, Repent and Recite

Decide, repent, and recite. Decide to accept the Christian kingdom for our lives. Repent our sins asking for a loving, peaceful forgiveness. Recite the Father's Prayer, moving forward into an eternal life out of our dividing, hateful destruction.

Jesus in His wisdom concerned Himself with teaching about the Kingdom of God that awaits us. The Kingdom of God is the one we must choose to be a faithful steward of, right now. The bible tells many historical stories of kings and their kingdoms. There were good, faithful kings and there were evil, hateful kings. These are our present day realities as well.

We have a Kingdom portion which is everything we choose it to be. We can choose our royal family just as much as we can choose our decrees. God has given His children a portion of His Kingdom to steward. We are in stewardship of our piece of the Kingdom, therefore; we need to continually assess how we steward our divine portion. The state of our Kingdom portion can affect the integrity of the entirety of God's Kingdom.

When we accept our Kingdom portion as a Christian, we must begin to realize the enormous opportunity that is being offered by our Loving Father in Heaven. Whether we are a janitor or an executive, we have the exact same opportunities within our Kingdom portion. We have the opportunity to attract the right people or the wrong people to reside amongst us. We can become very prosperous or very destitute. We can be exceedingly joyful or continually sorrowful. God has given us stewardship over His Kingdom, we only need to steward it well.

Jesus spent His entire ministry life, challenging us to become righteous servants, urging us to take advantage of this awesome gift. He even taught us how to make the right decisions, choosing to be sacrificed into an eternal Kingdom.

Jesus demonstrated such control over His Kingdom portion that He unmistakably proved God's resurrecting power. Proving that nothing in this world can stand in our way of living a holy righteous life for God, for we can stand in His service completely forgiven.

Others will want to dictate how we steward our Kingdom portion by demanding physical requirements to salvation that must be met. This is not what Jesus died upon the cross for. Jesus died so we can be free from the bondage of sinful transgressions. He revealed to us that if we have faith and faith alone, God is just to forgive our sins.

Repentance is a choice that we need to make in order to be welcomed by God's grace. Jesus Christ is our example of salvation, teaching repentance as the way to God's protective blessings. Our Kingdom portion will be free of torment if we first choose not to be tormented by insecurity. Our physical life, the whole experience, is under our entire control. We must choose the saving God.

When anyone decides to follow God wholeheartedly, it is proven throughout scripture, they will be blessed continuously.

By choosing God we align with all His children regardless the state of their Kingdom portion. Everyone that breathes life upon this beautiful planet deserves equal, attentive consideration. God demands we as Christians fulfill our duty to love everyone unconditionally. Our health depends on accepting every child of God, loving them accordingly.

If we harbor feelings of hateful resentment, our soul will never know God's peaceful love. We deny ourselves the blessing of good health when we judge another child of God. Whether lost or not, believer or unbeliever, we are all sheep in God's flock.

Jesus demands we wear our souls on our naked arms for all to see. We spend far too much energy dressing ourselves up as Christians. Many of us wear our Sunday costumes, falling prey to meaningless physical virtues. We become more concerned with observing traditional customs than obediently submitting to God. We are more concerned with performing in a role for the approval of others. Many of us are doing the exact opposite of what our Most Glorious Lord has endeavored to teach us. As Christians we are sometimes so far removed from the teachings of Christ that we lose our direction. Living in the truth becomes the last thing we concern ourselves with. Sacrificing nothing, while leaving no generational landmarks for others reference. Instead, we choose to spend our efforts judging others who do not meet our customary, traditional requirements.

Prayer

Prayer is the most important part of living a spiritual life. Some of our churches have placed too many controls on out prayer life, making in an ineffective worship tool. Jesus warns us not to fall into vain repetitions. Prayer is to be a personal, intimate experience with our Living God. With this being said, we must not allow our prayer be full of empty babbling for the performance pleasure of others.

Prayer is to be a different experience for each one of us. Prayer is meant to be an open communication with our Loving Father, not a controlled transaction. Churches need to allow room for free expression when concerning their congregation's prayer life. We then must respond in kind with a measure of obedience allowing God's word to saturate our hearts.

Jesus wants us to be successfully fulfilled through our prayer time with Him. We must never be afraid of being specific when praying for blessing or direction. When we focus our prayerful desires, God gives justly according to our faith. If we do not receive our desires, we must petition God, searching as to whether our commitment to Him has been faithful.

Unanswered prayer may be corrected by seeking first forgiveness. Jesus Christ teaches us that this is a fundamental part of prayer. If we desire to use Christ as our conduit blessing unto the Father, we must sacrifice our selfishness. What an example of selflessness we have in the image of Christ, the one true living example of forgiveness.

Forgiveness is a stumbling block that we must resolve ourselves to claim victory over, either by offering it or seeking it. Forgiveness goes far beyond the simple word "sorry", it is an overwhelming outpouring from within the depths of our heart. Once we have searched our hearts, we can only then continue in prayerful pursuit of our desires.

Approaching God in prayer with a heart of prejudice against a group of people drowns out our prayerful desires. We are to clean or sanctify our minds and souls before God. Doing this enables true revelation while encouraging power in prayer.

Fasting

God loves us, wanting to give His faithful children their desired blessings. If we still are not fulfilled in prayer, we must pursue God through fasting. Jesus places great importance on the measure of fasting. He encourages us to do it in secret, not allowing others to see our fasting. When we fast we must do so until we are fulfilled.

By fasting we will find a resolution to our soul issues. Fasting reinforces the power of the spiritual life over the vain pleasures of the flesh. Our flesh encourages many distractions in our life, fasting is our way of restoring the spiritual victory over our physical nature. Our spirit, when focused on the One True God, will always win over our flesh. Jesus proved this position through His most glorious resurrection. The soul, when handed over to Christ, carries over into eternal life.

Fasting is an individual spiritual need. No one can determine a specific custom or observance. To some, fasting may mean an abstention from certain stressful thoughts or emotions. To others, it may mean a physical fast of food or drink until fulfilled. In chronic cases, it means complete abstention of all worldly distractions, both physical and emotional.

Fasting is a tool to be used to quiet us before God, focusing on Him alone. Fasting in simplicity, is saying no to our physical desires while saying yes to God. God will direct us in our fast, making it a completely fulfilling time.

Focus

Our life's focus must be on God alone. We must not allow ourselves to be overcome with the distraction or desire to accumulate material prosperity. When we focus on God, He will provide according to our faith. He will not provide more than we are capable of faithfully stewarding.

Some churches are being deceived by the material prosperity of this world, ignoring the teachings of Jesus. Too many times we see churches adorn enormous buildings, all the while the homeless sleep in their dark shadows.

If we all sought truth rather than possessions, maybe our churches would follow our lead. The only thing we take into eternity is our faith. The only thing that compels positive change in us is faith in God.

Our lives must be focused on obtaining significant spiritual understanding, not selfish material gain. Focusing on God allows us to bring our physical desires into alignment with our spiritual experience. God will bless us with unmatchable physical prosperity, only if we seek him first.

Fulfillment

Through prayer we bring ourselves to God. In prayer we live an inward spiritual life full of peaceful happiness. Possessions bring our life focus outward into the flesh.

Our whole being is a spiritual one. God designed us in His likeness and image. We will never be content seeking fulfillment by satisfying the lusts of the flesh, only by living an inward searching life will our souls be satisfied. We must allow God to direct our soul to affect our physical environment. We must never allow our physical environment to direct the course of our soul.

God will speak to our soul while affecting our life in such a way that mountains of fear will be removed. Our fears of poverty will melt away, fear of betrayal dispersed, all our carnal fears will be cast away. All we must do is commit our souls to God's leadership, allowing our soul to determine our physical experiences.

God will speak to us in a whisper, so gentle we will miss it if we are living a life of the flesh. God is a faithful director with a faint voice telling us to help someone in need, a loving prod to step out of our comfort zone. If we seek God, He is faithful in answering our calling. Through serving God in this way we will finally live in peaceful freedom.

We must not live in the future, yearning to be in the tomorrow that never comes. We must live each present moment as a gift from God. We must live to make a Godly impression today in this very present moment. We have the divine ability to move nations if only we opened our inner being to the working of the Holy Spirit.

Judgment

Judgmental attitudes have no place within a spirit-filled Christian church. Jesus condemns it, laying out a three-fold doctrinal teaching specifically directed at judging others.

First, when we judge another it brings us to a very serious open sin. Judging another places us on the throne of authority, designated only for our Holy God. Too many times we try to assume the role of our Most Glorious Lord, elevating ourselves to His judgmental authority. In doing this, we put ourselves in great peril of challenging God's sovereignty. God will quickly humble judgmental people, as He is the only one mandated to judge His children.

Second, judging each other will break the connection of God's blessing of peace. When we judge another we are assuming there is nothing good in that person, or group of people, to rejoice in the Lord about. When we see no good in another, we see no good in God. We are all divine creations ensuring that we all have the potential to be amazing Godly witnesses. We need to appreciate God's ability to use anyone He wishes to witness to the world.

Third, when we judge others we condemn ourselves to the same judgment. Every ill word said about another, will be returned likewise to us. If we want to live peacefully amongst the nations, we must learn to cast our judgments far from our mind when tempted.

These are the doctrinal teachings of our Lord and Savior Jesus Christ. At no time, under no circumstance are we permitted to judge another child of God. Those who do will answer for it in eternity.

Motives

If we find ourselves hurt after doing something nice or helpful because we received no thankful praise, then we did it for the reward of praise, not to glorify God as a witness for Him. This teaching prepares us regarding the eternal perspective of our works unto the Lord. For it is not by works we will gain entry into heaven, therefore; why should we continue in works for the reward of praise. We should have a desire to fulfill our call, seeking nothing in return except completion of the appointed task.

We must not just learn to bite our tongue, instead; we must change how we think. We must think of others, as we would want them to think of us. Our actions and words will align with our thoughts. We will not answer for our thoughts in an earthly court, however; we will in our heavenly court. Adopt a loving, peaceful mindset today in order to escape eternal judgment in the future.

Witnessing

The condition of our fruit will reveal the true spiritual self. Jesus relates the worth of our works to a conditional fruit. If our works bring glory to God aligning to His will, our fruit will be good. If our works bring glory to ourselves aligning to our own desires, our fruit will be sour. When good fruit ripens, it will fall from the branch carrying life giving seed, planting itself allowing for multiplication.

In the course of witnessing the Gospel to others, we must keep this teaching in mind. We must strive to produce good fruit that will carry good seed so that it may multiply. We must allow God to guide us according to His willful nourishment. He opens doors that allow us to witness the life giving gospel to others. We must petition Him in prayer, every day seeking His glorious face and divine direction.

Not everyone we come to know is open or ready for the Gospel presentation, as they are not ready to submit to a Christian life. In this situation, our Christian life will be all the Godly witness we need offer. Attempting to openly visit the Gospel with these people pushes them further from God. These people need to see the spiritual life in action. We cannot show them the benefit of a spiritual Christ-filled life if we are not living one. Our spiritual Christ-filled life should example a peaceful love of all God's children.

When God presents an opening in our conversations to share the Gospel, we are obligated to do so. Sharing the Gospel without God's leading is careless, as well; counterproductive. Living out a Christ-filled life will impress upon pre-Christians the desire to have the life God has given us as Christians.

Bible

We must endeavor to read our Bibles with an open mind, no longer limiting God's wisdom to a carnal experience. Reading the Bible should be a spiritual experience that is open to the leading of the Holy Spirit.

We are all mere children of God, all of us siblings adopted into God's family. No one is greater than the other within this family. We must all look to the Father for ultimate protection. When we acknowledge the Bible as God's eternal love letter of instruction to His children, our spiritual understanding will grow exponentially.

The Bible is a living entity that is always relevant now and forever. When we pursue God through the reading of His eternal love letter, we find strength. Strength that will give us encouragement to continue the active pursuit of His directed will for our lives.

We must pursue God by storming the very gates of Heaven. We must no longer starve the Holy Spirit by neglecting our soulful need to know God through His scriptures. God has appointed us heirs to both His eternal and present-day Kingdoms. For too long we have been living for eternity, focusing on tomorrow instead of today.

Surrender

The harvest is plentiful in souls and prosperity. We must pursue blessings of health, wealth, happiness, family and forgiveness. We must pursue the blessings God has made accessible to us. If we reorganize our priorities allowing for prayerful meditation, God will lead us to all the good fruit we can handle.

Jesus teaches us that an inner submission is of far more importance than an outer submission. The inward life is founded on humility with every step harder than the last, allowing every moment to echo into eternity. The outward life is founded on pride with every step easier than the last, allowing every moment to be lost forever. Refusing to submit our soul to God will leave us feeling unfulfilled, never able to reach our expected potential.

God wants great things for us; He also demands great faith to get us there. Every prayer is answered according to the amount of faith one has. If we believe in God, handing entire control of our soul over to Him, prosperous things will happen.

Jesus is the most profound and simplistic teacher the world has ever known. His teachings resonate with the truth of God for the simple fact they work. In application, the teachings of Christ result in prosperous blessing.

Potential

Truth heals the sick, cleanses the soul, and solves life's difficulties. This teaching of Christ has been proven to be infallible, as well; practical through demonstration. When we surround ourselves with truth we build a fortress of protection around us. The truth will always be our tool to navigate our souls deeper into God's Kingdom of blessing.

God has given His children according to their faith, the ability to cast out demons, perform merciful healings and speak through tongues. God has given us dominion over our outward lives. He wants us to reign over our here-and-now Kingdom Portion as righteous heirs.

Once we realize the potential awaiting us, we are compelled to perform spiritually. Our progress may be slow, however; as long as we are moving forward we are performing. Our lives have become hardened by spiritual doubt and religious mistrust. We must allow the forward movement of God to break down our hardness. We need to focus more on the spiritual moments of life rather than the physical minutes that distract us from our calling.

False Prophets

False prophets will erect stumbling blocks in the name of Religion. We must recognize these blockades in order to overcome them by way of the mighty power of the Lord. We must never sidestep from our directed path, always challenging them in the name of Jesus Christ.

False teachers are the agents of satan, desiring that every believer will become distracted. Once a believer is distracted the enemy can then divide them from the strength of God's fellowship. As soon as the believer is divided from the protection of God, satan will devour every last morsel of excited joy they may have left for the Lord's Kingdom. When the false prophet is finished his task, the believer will be filled with a desolate disappointment.

False teachers will set out disciples of destruction upon this earth, teaching all manner of hateful judgment. They will endeavor to add poison to the living water that springs forth from a true Christian witness. We must be always on guard as faithful warriors in the service of Christ.

We must never allow anybody or anything to come between our desire to seek God. No man, woman, or institution can be allowed to become a stumbling block. Me must remain vigilant in the liberty of our soul. We do not owe loyalty to anyone or thing except the Holy Trinity.

Reflection

Our walk with God is one of a kind. No one else will have the exact same experiences, only similar ones. If we want an indication of our own spiritual progress, we need only take a step back and look at the condition of our private life.

If we are living out Godly principles we will have success, or at the very least improvement. If our fruit be good, our soul is right with God. Likewise, if our fruit be sour, our soul is in need of God.

Our physical reverence is of no concern to God. God demands our spiritual loyalty. When we submit our soul to God all other dimensions of our life become pleasing in His sight. Only by being in the constant presence of God will we know lasting change. Nothing will ever fulfill a faithful Christian unless it is of God. Everything else is superficial and fragile.

One could say it is better to have never heard the Truth, than to know of it and never try to live it. Seek first the witness that which is Christ Jesus.

www.ingramcontent.com/pod-product-compliance
Ingram Content Group UK Ltd.
Pitfield, Milton Keynes, MK11 3LW, UK
UKHW020219250726
13967UKWH00001B/84

9 781304 701848